CONTENTS

Acknowledgements   4

Introduction   5

Donnybrook Then & Now   6

About the Author & Photographer   96

ACKNOWLEDGEMENTS

A variety of sources have been used to procure the old images of Donnybrook and I am grateful to Danny Parkinson and his family for giving me access to the Parkinson collection, most of which is housed in the National Library of Ireland. My thanks to the chairman, committee and members of the Ballsbridge, Donnybrook and Sandymount Historical Society, for their help and encouragement. I also wish to acknowledge the help given to me by Liz Turley and Angela O'Connell, librarians at Pembroke Library. My thanks, too, to the staff in the Gilbert Library in Pearse Street, in particular to Dr Maire Kennedy, Dr Mary Clark and Eithne Massey. In addition, Anne Henderson and the staff of the Irish Architectural Archive have been very helpful and supportive of my research. Honora Fall and the staff of the National Library have been more than willing to help me. Louise Canavan (Pharmaceutical Society of Ireland) was very helpful in relation to the history of Woodside, Shrewsbury Road. My thanks too, to the archivist at the Royal Automobile Club, Bob Montgomery. Gerard Whelan and the staff of the RDS Library have facilitated my research in every way possible. Thank you to Patricia McKenna for information on Mount Eden Road. Drs Donal and Frances Costigan gave me access to their private residence for which I am grateful. Councillor Dermot Lacey very kindly gave me access to his collection of images of Donnybrook. I am also grateful to the owners and previous owners of the shops and businesses in Donnybrook, as well as the people of Donnybrook in general, who shared their memories and photographs of Donnybrook with me.

The modern high-quality photographs of Donnybrook for this book are the work of Vincent Clarke, my co-author, with whom it has been a pleasure to work. I also wish to express our thanks to Beth Amphlett our editor, and to Ronan Colgan of The History Press Ireland for all their support and advice.

Unless otherwise specified, all the archive images are from my collection. Every effort has been made to identify the copyright holders of the old images and acknowledgements given. Should a source not be acknowledged correctly the necessary amendment will be made at the first opportunity.

INTRODUCTION

Donnybrook is one of Dublin's most iconic villages. Donnybrook or Domnach Broch, the Church of Broc (or the Church of the Badger), may date back to the eighth century, when St Broc is reputed to have built a convent in Donnybrook on the site of the present Graveyard.

Over the centuries Donnybrook also became well known for the famous Donnybrook Fair, which existed for over 700 years. The site of the fairground is the present-day Bective and Old Wesley Rugby Clubs, but it also stretched across the road to where Donnybrook Lawn Tennis Club is located today. The Fair Green is also close to Donnybrook Graveyard as popular gatherings for many centuries were associated with burial grounds.

The nineteenth and twentieth centuries were a time when the growth of suburbs took place not only in Dublin but in other European cities as well. It was a time of social migration, when wealthy inhabitants of the city of Dublin moved to the newly developed suburbs. Cities were seen as the harbinger of disease and the wealthy citizens of Dublin were keen to move to suburbia with its fine houses and villas. The fashionable Dublin suburbs were initially focused on the Pembroke and Rathmines Townships, both of which were located very close to the city centre. The growth and development of the south-side suburbs, in particular, was driven by businessmen and property developers, or by independent landowners like the Earl of Pembroke.

Donnybrook was part of the Pembroke Township that from 1863 onwards included Ballsbridge, Donnybrook, Sandymount, Irishtown and Ringsend. Large houses and villas of quality were the hallmark of the Pembroke Township, and Donnybrook acquired its fair share of leafy roads, large houses and villas, which were built on land leased from the Pembroke Estate. At this time there was a sizeable working-class population in the Pembroke Township and lack of adequate housing was a major problem. The provision of housing for artisans in the Pembroke Township was spearheaded by the Pembroke Estate. In 1912 eighty-eight artisan dwellings were built in Donnybrook beside Herbert Park. The majority of the houses were in Home Villas, and St Broc's Cottages was also part of this development.

The focus of this book is on the physical environment of Donnybrook, its major buildings, fine houses and streetscapes in general. Great changes have taken place in the streetscapes of Donnybrook over the centuries, and this book endeavours to show these changes with images of Donnybrook as it was then and as it is now.

AILESBURY ROAD

AILESBURY ROAD DATES from the nineteenth century, when the south Dublin suburbs were developed.
The road is named for the Marquis of Ailesbury, who was a son-in-law of the Earl of Pembroke. There were a number of different builders involved in the development of the road, including Michael Meade, and William Wardrop. One of the main builders was Michael Meade, who built St Michael's, now a school, as his family home. This was modelled on Queen Victoria's favourite residence, Osborne, on the Isle of Wight. Meade also built Nos 1–19 Ailesbury Road. His firm was famous for the quality of their workmanship, and for their quality houses, constructed of red brick and granite. Traditionally, diplomatic missions and embassies have been located on Ailesbury Road, perhaps the most famous being the residence of the French Ambassador at No. 53, formerly known as Mytilene.

KNOWN AS ONE of the most expensive roads in Dublin, Ailesbury Road's houses are still sold for several millions of euro every year. It is often called the Golden Mile! Besides private residences, it houses diplomatic missions and embassies, as it did in times past. As in the 1901 and 1911 Census, this road continues to be home to a number of professional families, doctors, lawyers and businessmen. More modern houses and

apartments are to be found at the Donnybrook end of Ailesbury Road. Some of these were built in the grounds of an old house known at various times as St Ann's or Annville. Another historic house in the grounds of the present-day St Ann's Apartments was formerly known as Lilliput, and is now called Riversdale. It was home to Arthur Morrison, a former Lord Mayor of Dublin whose obelisk stands at the junction of Ailesbury and Anglesea roads.

AN ÓIGE
HOSTEL

AN ÓIGE IS an Irish Youth Hostelling Association which was founded on 7 May 1931 by Dr Thekla Beere (1902-1991). A distinguished civil servant, she chaired the United Nations Commission on the Status of Women in 1970. She was also Secretary General of the Department of Transport and Power.

The headquarters of An Óige are located in Dublin at 61 Mountjoy Street. An Óige, operates a number of youth hostels in Ireland, some of which are only open in the summer. The An Óige Hostel on Morehampton Road opened in 1956 and it closed in 1989. The hostel contained 100 beds and had been established with the aid of a grant from the National Development Fund. It seems to have operated without any major problems over the years. The premises were re-decorated in 1957 and had major fire precaution improvements in 1984. The long-standing and popular wardens of this

An Óige Hostel were Mr and Mrs J. Colgan. An Óige had arrangements with the school next door whereby An Óige took over some classrooms at the school for the overflow of hostelers during the summer season. During the winter season, the school (Park House and later Rosemount School) could use some of the hostel's facilities.

TODAY THE FORMER premises of An Óige are known as Morehampton Town House, and contain an up-market bed and breakfast. The building dates back to the 1860s and still contains interesting architectural features including fine cornices. The first occupant listed in *Thom's Directory* was Revd Thomas Stack, Registrar of Trinity College Dublin. Another distinguished resident was John Radcliffe, a former Pro-Vice-Chancellor of TCD and a founding member of the Institute of Engineers. For a number of years (1875 until 1923). it was a select boarding school for young girls.

BEAVER ROW

BEAVER ROW HAS been in existence since at least 1813. It acquired its name from a beaver hat factory that was located on the opposite side of the River Dodder during the early nineteenth century. It is not clear when the factory closed, but it was still in existence in 1826, when the Wright brothers were in charge. The Wright brothers were very good to their employees, who came from the north of England and were Wesleyan Methodist. They built cottages, a Wesleyan Methodist Church, a school, a hall, and a wooden bridge over the Dodder for their employees. A house called Beech Hill, off Beaver Row, belonged to one of the Wright brothers. The First All-Ireland Football final between teams from Limerick and Dundalk was played at Beech Hill in 1882. Beaver Row was often known as Suzy Row because of the number of women who ran washing and mangling businesses from their homes here. *(Image courtesy of Danny Parkinson; Keogh's Dairy Farm image courtesy of Danny Parkinson)*

TODAY, THE COTTAGES built by the Wright brothers on Beaver Row are still in existence, though many of them have been modernised to cater for twenty-first-century living. The Wesleyan Methodist church is still there too, and is to be found in the back garden of No. 9 Beaver Row. The present owner of the house and church is an American writer, who has been instrumental in acquiring a preservation order on the church. The old school house and hall built by the Wright brothers were demolished in recent years, and replaced by modern houses and apartments called Fisherman's Wharf. Two dairy farms which existed until the 1970s on Beaver Row have been replaced by David Lloyd's Riverview, a modern sports complex with indoor and outdoor tennis courts, an indoor and outdoor swimming pool, squash courts, and a high-quality gym. Riverview provides excellent sports facilities for individuals, families and children.

BECTIVE RANGERS RUGBY CLUB AND OLD WESLEY RUGBY CLUB

BECTIVE RANGERS RUGBY Club was founded in 1881. It began as Bective Football Club, founded by former pupils of Bective House Seminary for Young Gentlemen (1834) and located at 15 Rutland Square East (Parnell Square). The school closed in 1885, and membership of the Rugby Club was opened to non Bective past pupils. It was then re-named Bective Rangers Football Club. From the beginning, Bective was always a major force in Irish rugby. In 1889, it won the Leinster Senior Cup, and since then it has added many club and national trophies to its credit. Bective RFC played rugby on a number of grounds around the city, including the Phoenix Park, until it moved to Donnybrook and the old Fair Green in the 1900s. *(Image courtesy of Danny Parkinson)*

PAST PUPILS OF Wesley College, Dublin, founded old Wesley Rugby Club in 1891. The Club moved to Donnybrook during the 1919/20 rugby season. Like Bective RFC, Old Wesley has produced a substantial number of international rugby players. They share the grounds at Donnybrook with Bective Rugby Club and these grounds are also the home of Leinster Rugby. There has been a general upgrading of the facilities at Donnybrook in recent years, including a new stand for rugby fans. Another club located in the same grounds is Bective Tennis Club, founded over ninety years ago. It was originally a part of Bective Rugby Club, but in 1921 it became a separate entity with seven tennis courts on the banks of the River Dodder. The Dodder has overflown its banks on numerous occasions, and the tennis courts have suffered accordingly (in particular, during Hurricane Charley in 1986, when the tennis courts were completely flooded and had to be resurfaced). New all-weather courts have been installed in recent years enabling members to play tennis all year round.

13

BEECH HILL

A HOUSE THAT no longer exists was Beech Hill House, which was built in the nineteenth century. It belonged to Joseph Wright, a member of the family who built the hat factory on Beaver Row. The house was located at the entrance to the present Beech Hill Estate. There was also a lodge at the entrance to Beech Hill House, and the last occupants of this lodge were a family called Ennis. During the Second World War, a knitting factory operated in this house. For many years, up the late 1970s, Dublin Corporation provided chalets/caravans for elderly people to live in where Beech Hill Court now stands. In the early years many of the residents availed of the facilities of the Hammond Lane Social Club, which operated from where David Lloyd's Riverview now stands. The closing of the Hammond Lane Social Club was a major loss to the residents of Beech Hill, and the area in general. *(Image courtesy of David Crampton)*

TODAY, THE SITE of Beech Hill House is occupied by Beech Hill Flats, built by Crampton's for Dublin Corporation in the 1960s. Re-housing families from the poor housing conditions in Dublin city centre was a major issue during the 1950s. The Beech Hill Estate was built in tandem with a very progressive scheme developed by the Irish Glass Bottle Company (located in Ringsend) for their employees. The complex at Beech Hill Terrace, popularly known as 'The Maisonettes', is in a very poor state of repair today. Planning is at advanced stage that will see the Royal Hospital Donnybrook Voluntary Housing Association taking them over. A major rebuild and refurbishment will then ensue. In recent years, individual tenants have purchased many of the Corporation houses and flats in Beech Hill. It is now a thriving community with a wonderful Community Association.

15

BELFIELD
HOUSE

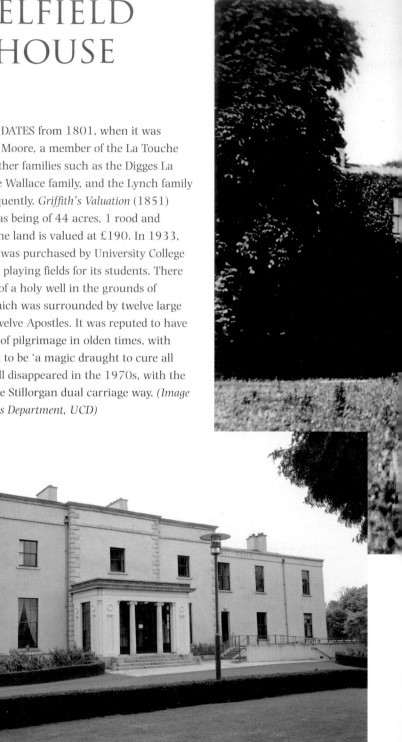

BELFIELD HOUSE DATES from 1801, when it was
built for Ambrose Moore, a member of the La Touche
banking family. Other families such as the Digges La
Touche family, the Wallace family, and the Lynch family
occupied it subsequently. *Griffith's Valuation* (1851)
describes Belfield as being of 44 acres, 1 rood and
25 perches, and the land is valued at £190. In 1933,
the Belfield estate was purchased by University College
Dublin, to provide playing fields for its students. There
was evidence too of a holy well in the grounds of
Belfield House, which was surrounded by twelve large
trees called the Twelve Apostles. It was reputed to have
been a holy place of pilgrimage in olden times, with
the water believed to be 'a magic draught to cure all
ailments'. The well disappeared in the 1970s, with the
development of the Stillorgan dual carriage way. *(Image
courtesy of Archives Department, UCD)*

IN 1960, THE Government agreed that University College Dublin (UCD) could move all its faculties from Earlsfort Terrace, in the city, out to Belfield. In 1964, the Faculty of Science buildings were the first to be completed and today Belfield House is one of the eight historic houses that were purchased by UCD to form their main campus. Nowadays, Belfield House is home to the Clinton Institute for American Studies, which was established in 2003. Today UCD is the largest of the Irish universities with over 30,000 students drawn from up to 124 different countries. The grounds at Belfield consist of 133 hectares, with woodland walks and magnificent mature grounds, making it a beautiful, leafy modern university campus. It is interesting to note that Belfield was one of the original sites suggested for Dublin Airport.

BELMONT AVENUE

BELMONT AVENUE WAS originally known as Coldblow Lane, but its name was changed to Belmont Avenue in the 1840s. Coldblow Lane originally led up to Coldblow House, owned by a Colonel Coldblow. The grounds are now part of Milltown Park, home of the Jesuit Fathers, and the Milltown Institute. During the 1780s this house was the home of Sir William Fortick, and later, home to the Hon. Denis George Coldblow. Members of the Roberts family also lived in Coldblow House. Captain Lewis Riall of Old Conna was a descendant of the Roberts family and he was responsible for building a number of houses on Mount Eden Road and Morehampton Road. Belmont House (*c*. 1760), close to Sandford Road, is one of the oldest houses on the road. The majority of the houses on Belmont Avenue date from the 1860s and 1870s. However, some of the redbrick terraces of houses are later, dating from the 1880s and the 1900s. (*Image courtesy of Bob Montgomery, RAC Archivist*)

TODAY BELMONT AVENUE is a busy thoroughfare linking Morehampton Road with Sandford Road. A number of the terraces of red-brick houses are still in excellent condition, and one of the terraces still bears the name Aberdeen Terrace, named for the Lord Lieutenant Lord Aberdeen. Another terrace of twelve houses was called Stella Terrace and it is located half way up the road on the right-hand side as you go towards Sandford Road. Another named terrace is called Newport Terrace, built by John Newport, a grocer from Morehampton Road. The Royal Irish Constabulary (RIC) barracks was located behind O'Connell's restaurant on Morehampton Road, in an area formerly known as Belmont Court. Over the years this area has housed a number of different restaurants such as the very popular Courtyard and later Tenors. Today, it is occupied by Marco Pierre White's new restaurant.

BLOOMFIELD HOUSE

IN 1811, THE Religious Society of Friends (Quakers) acquired Bloomfield House. That same year saw the opening of Bloomfield Hospital, to provide mental health and nursing care for the elderly, and for those suffering from dementia. Prior to this, Bloomfield House belonged to William Saurin (1757–1839), a distinguished Irish lawyer, who was bitterly opposed to the Act of Union. He became a member for Blessington, in the Irish House of Commons, to combat the Union. He was offered the post of Solicitor General in 1798, but he turned it down. Despite this, in the early nineteenth century he was appointed Attorney General, and was very much against Catholic Emancipation. He sold Bloomfield House in 1802 to Dr Robert Emmet, the father of Robert Emmet, the nineteenth-century patriot, and Thomas Addis Emmet. Dr Robert Emmet was physician to St Patrick's Hospital (Swift's Hospital). The Emmet family continued to own Bloomfield House after the death of Dr Robert Emmet, and the family sold it in 1809, for £1,520, to the Society of Friends. *(Image courtesy of the Society of Friends)*

TODAY, BLOOMFIELD HOUSE stands empty and awaits restoration. Part of its grounds and those of Swanbrook house have been redeveloped as Edward Square. In 2005, the Society of Friends moved Bloomfield Hospital, Swanbrook and Westfield from Donnybrook to Stocking Lane in Rathfarnham. Now known as Bloomfield Health Services, it is a not-for-profit healthcare provider. There, it continues to take care of those with mental health problems and the new premises and facilities provides a state-of-the-art environment for the care and treatment of elderly patients, and those with psychiatric problems in general. The services offered at Bloomfield Health Services are based on the Quaker ethos and principles of care, dignity, compassion and social justice.

CHURCH OF THE SACRED HEART

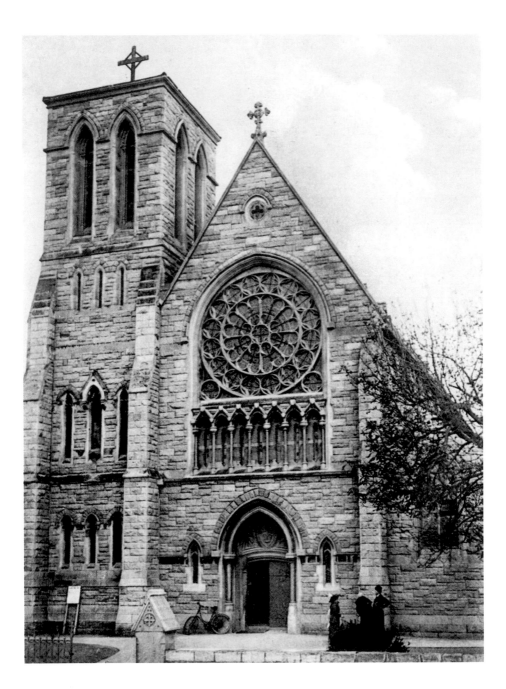

THE FORERUNNER OF the Church of the Sacred Heart was the old Catholic church dedicated to St Mary, located in Donnybrook Graveyard, beside Donnybrook's Protestant church; it dated back to 1795. Over the years, the Catholic Church fell into decay and a new church was required to replace the old one. Monsignor Andrew O'Connell became parish priest of the combined parishes of Donnybrook, Irishtown, Ringsend and Sandymount in 1849, and he was responsible for building new churches in Sandymount, Ringsend and Donnybrook.

The architects for the Church of the Sacred Heart were Pugin and Ashlin and Michael Meade was the builder. W. & J. Bolger built the extensions in the 1930s. Cardinal Paul Cullen, Archbishop of Dublin, officially opened the new church in 1866, and it was dedicated to the Sacred Heart. Interesting architectural features include a rose window, and beautiful stained-glass windows by Harry Clarke and Michael Healy.

THE CHURCH OF the Sacred Heart today is one of the wealthiest parishes in the Archdioceses of Dublin. It is a large parish, extending from the south side of Ranelagh Road to the RDS in Ballsbridge and from Belfield, the home of University College Dublin, almost to Leeson Street Bridge. Today the parish is organised by the parish council which has been in existence since 2006 and meets every month. There are a number of active parish groups today, such as Alcoholics Anonymous, Donnybrook Neighbours, Aware Support Groups, Donnybrook Youth Club, the Legion of Mary, the Mary Aikenhead Day Centre, the St Pio of Pietrelcina Prayer Group, the Donnybrook Active Retirement Group, the Eucharistic Adoration Group, the Small Christian Community, and the parish choir.

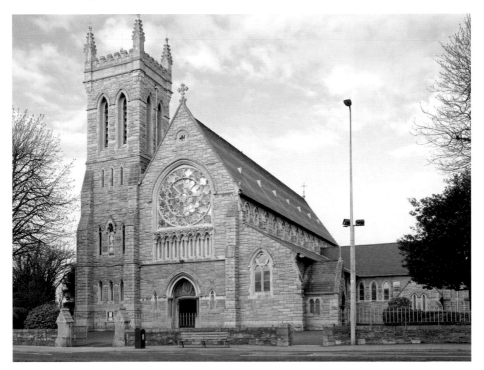

CRAMPTON-BUILT HOUSES

CRAMPTON'S ARE ONE of the longest established and best-known builders in Dublin. The firm dates from 1879, when George J. Crampton founded it. Crampton's nephew Tom joined the company in 1907 and from then it was known as G. & T. Crampton. There are many Crampton-built houses in Donnybrook, especially those on Herbert Park, Argyle Road, Arranmore Road and Brendan Road, which have more than stood the test of time. Crampton's built these houses between 1909 and 1929. Some of the most iconic buildings in Dublin have also been built by G. & T. Crampton, from the UCD building in Earlsfort Terrace, now the National Concert Hall, to the United States Embassy in Ballsbridge and not forgetting the International Financial Services Centre. *(Image courtesy of David Crampton)*

CRAMPTON-BUILT HOUSES are built to a very high standard, and they continue to be in demand as family homes. Perhaps one of the most interesting houses built by Crampton's is No. 32 Herbert Park, built for T.A. (Alfred) Fannin, managing director of Fannin's Medical and Surgical Suppliers. Detailed specifications for materials to be used in building the

house, and instructions regarding the quality of the workmanship required, extended to ten pages. The management and staff of G. & T. Crampton have always taken great pride in their work. A Crampton house is synonymous with quality, and is a highly desirable residence. House building is not the only aspect of building in which Crampton's are involved in today. They are experts not only in new buildings, extensions and expansions; they also carry out refurbishments and the fitting-out of complex heritage buildings. Over the centuries they have built, and continue to build, commercial, retail, leisure, social, educational and industrial buildings of the highest quality. *(Image courtesy of Danny Parkinson)*

DODDER RIVER

UNTIL THE EIGHTEENTH century, there was a ford over the River Dodder at Donnybrook. The first bridge was built in 1741, but it was swept away by a flood. There were a number of other bridges over the river until the present bridge, the Anglesey Bridge, was built in 1832. It is named for Henry Paget, 1st Marquis of Anglesea (1768–1854), who was Lord Lieutenant at the time. During the nineteenth century, millraces, millponds and weirs were constructed on the Dodder to harness its power for industrial purposes. Among the industries found on the Dodder at Donnybrook were paper mills, cloth mills, iron mills, corn mills and bleach mills. Some of the early maps show a windmill near where Eglinton Terrace now stands. Flooding has always been a problem along the Dodder over the years – Hurricane Charley caused major damage to property along the river in 1986. Prior to that, two major floods occurred, in 1905 and in 1931, when the river overflowed its banks, causing horrendous damage to private houses and gardens. *(Image courtesy of Danny Parkinson)*

TREMENDOUS IMPROVEMENTS HAVE taken place over the years regarding the River Dodder as an amenity, with new paths along its banks, and the river regularly cleaned up by volunteers organised by the Dodder Action Group. Wildlife today along the Dodder includes birds such as mallards, grey herons, kingfishers, etc. Foxes are frequently seen along its riverbanks and badgers have also been found there. There is also evidence that a small feral population of mandarin duck are to be found on it. An Irish Wildlife Trust survey of 2013 found otters living along the river. Today there are some really delightful walks along the banks of the river. The Dodder is a popular venue for fishing, and the season (which requires a permit) is from 17 March to 30 September each year.

DONNYBROOK BUSES
AND DONNYBROOK
BUS GARAGE

SINCE BUSES WERE first introduced in Dublin, Donnybrook has always had its designated bus numbers – Nos 9 and 10 – and the origin of these numbers went back to the trams. It was with great regret that the people of Donnybrook saw these historic bus routes disappear. Thankfully, the No. 46A bus is still with us; it cannot properly be called a Donnybrook bus, as its destination from the centre of town is Dún Laoghaire. Nowadays we also have the No. 39A and No. 145 buses, which pass through Donnybrook on their way to various destinations in the city. Donnybrook, however, is bereft of its own specifically numbered buses, as they have now passed into history. This is not the first time that the No. 10 bus has been abolished, and with a bit of luck Donnybrook will get its own specific numbered bus back again! *(Image courtesy of Michael Pegum; No. 10 bus image courtesy of Dublin Bus)*

DONNYBROOK BUS GARAGE was built on the site of an old quarry. The present bus garage dates from 1952. Michael Scott, the well-known Irish architect, in association with the Danish engineer Ove Arup, designed it. It is an iconic building, with a preservation order on it. It was 'the first building in the world to have a concrete shell roof lit by natural light from one end to the other'. It is uninterrupted by columns or internal walls. It was used by 1955 for an international boxing match when Billy Kelly, from Derry, was defeated by Ray Famechon of France. Today the bus garage can accommodate up to sixty buses in ten parking bays. In more recent years improvements have been made to the accommodation and staff amenities in the garage. This included a new administration building, an improved vehicle servicing building and the provision of new pits and servicing equipment. Facilities for staff now included a new canteen, a recreation room, showers and toilets.

DONNYBROOK CASTLE

MEMBERS OF THE Ussher family, who owned major pieces of land in Donnybrook, built Donnybrook Castle in the sixteenth century. The castle was an Elizabethan-style mansion, and continued in use for a number of centuries. In 1649 Oliver Cromwell is reputed to have selected Donnybrook Castle as a rendezvous for his army after he had taken the city of Drogheda. The beginning of the eighteenth century saw Donnybrook Castle vested with trustees for the purpose of sale. Sir Francis Stoyte, a Lord Mayor of Dublin in 1705, was one of the trustees, and for a while it was occupied by some of his relatives, including Jonathan Swift's friend Stella. Robert Jocelyn, who subsequently became Lord Chancellor of Ireland, bought the demesne and lands of Donnybrook Castle in 1726. By 1816 Donnybrook Castle had become a school for boys, and it was known as the Castle School. In 1837 it was purchased by Mother Mary Aikenhead as a home for the Religious Sisters of Charity and the Magdalene Home. *(Image courtesy of the National Library of Ireland)*

TODAY, THE SITE of Donnybrook Castle continues to be occupied by the Religious Sisters of Charity. The order was founded in December 1816, with the specific aim of serving the poor, and this continues to be its mission. It was founded by Mother Mary Aikenhead who was born a Protestant in Cork city. She converted to Catholicism and then became a nun, before founding her own congregation. Over the years the Religious Sisters of Charity in Donnybrook have run an asylum and laundry, as well as doing a great deal of work to help the poor of Donnybrook and surrounding areas. What may not be generally known is that Mother Mary Aikenhead is interred in the nuns' cemetery, which is located in the former gardens of Donnybrook Castle. A large memorial cross marks her grave.

DONNYBROOK FAIR

A ROYAL CHARTER of King John established the
Donnybrook Fair in 1204. It began as an important
livestock and produce market, but as the years went
by it became more of a carnival and funfair. Tolls and
taxes from the fair's activities were initially vested
in the Corporation of Dublin, but during the 1690s
the Corporation transferred the right to the revenues
from the fair to the Ussher family of Donnybrook.
In 1812, the right to the revenues of the fair passed
to the Madden family, who also lived in Donnybrook.
Food and drink were important elements of the fair,
and entertainment was available in abundance.
Over the centuries the fair became a byword for
drunkenness and carousing, and nights often ended up
in a free-for-all, with plenty of fighting among those
attending. During the mid-nineteenth century the fair
became a great nuisance and embarrassment to the
respectable people of Donnybrook, so a Committee for

the Abolition of the Donnybrook Fair was established. The Revd. P.J. Nolan, a curate in Donnybrook, managed to persuade a parishioner, Eleanor Madden, to part with the licence for £3,000 that had been raised by the Committee. When the Patent for the Fair was sold, a relative of the Madden family called Joseph Dillon had the lease and licence of a public house close to the old Fair Green. He took advantage of the abolition of the fair to revive it on his own ground. His version of the Donnybrook Fair came to an end on 26 August 1866, the day the new Church of the Sacred Heart was opened. *(Image courtesy of the National Library of Ireland)*

TODAY THE DONNYBROOK Fair is synonymous with a family-run gourmet food company owned by Mr Joe Doyle. The company also includes a cooking school, restaurant and catering services.

DONNYBROOK GRAVEYARD

THE CHURCH OF Ireland parish church of Donnybrook and the Catholic church were both located within the Graveyard. Both churches were named St Mary's. The Fitzwilliam family had a small chapel attached to the Protestant church, and members of their family were buried there. The first family member to be buried there was Sir Richard Fitzwilliam, who died in 1595. Other distinguished Irish men buried in this graveyard include Archbishop William King (1650–1729), Revd Richard Graves (1763–1829), Bartholomew Mosse (1712–1759), Richard Robert Madden (1798–1886), and Sir Edward Lovett Pearce (1699–1733). The last two burials in Donnybrook Graveyard were the two sisters of the Revd Gore Ryder, Elizabeth (d. 1935) and Amy (d. 1936).

Our knowledge of Donnybrook Graveyard has been greatly enhanced by the work of Danny Parkinson (author of *Donnybrook Graveyard*), the work carried out by volunteers, and a Department of Labour-funded Social Employment Scheme under the Chairmanship of Dermot Lacey, a former Lord Mayor of Dublin and a Labour Councillor. Cecil Harmsworth King and his wife Dame Ruth King were also involved in the project, and contributed financially to it. Julian Walton (Irish Genealogical Research Society) undertook the first systematic recording of all the monumental inscriptions. A complete list of 240 inscriptions is available in the sub-committee's archive in the Irish Genealogical Office. *(Image courtesy of* The Irish Times*)*

THE WALL DIVIDING the Graveyard today from the local Garda Station is the wall of the old Catholic church of St Mary. Today, the Graveyard is under the care of Dublin City Council. The Ballsbridge, Donnybrook and Sandymount Historical Society is involved in regular clean-up work of the Graveyard; this take place twice a year. Mr David Nearly, a local historian, conducts regular tours of Donnybrook Graveyard during the summer months.

DONNYBROOK
LAWN TENNIS CLUB

DONNYBROOK LAWN TENNIS Club dates back to 1893, making it one of Ireland's oldest tennis clubs. It was immediately a popular venue with the people of Donnybrook, and by September of 1893 the club had enrolled 147 members. The very first At Home was held in 1894, and it soon became a popular event at which to be seen – it often had an attendance of up to 800 people. In the early days of the club the tennis season was quite

short – it opened in early May, and ran through to mid or late September. The grounds were then used in winter by a hockey club, who rented the grounds from the tennis club.

The boundaries of Donnybrook Lawn Tennis Club are almost unchanged since the foundation of the club, with the exception of an extra piece of land acquired on the west side of its grounds in 1983. A millrace ran underground along the west and north side of Donnybrook Tennis Club in the nineteenth century, carrying water from the River Dodder to Johnston, Mooney & O'Brien's bakery in Ballsbridge. Water from the millrace has been known to have leaked, and it has damaged the tennis courts from time to time.

The club's first president was Mr Justice Madden, a member of the very well-known Donnybrook family. The Earl of Pembroke, who remained in office for nineteen years, succeeded him. Although from the outset ladies and gentlemen members were regarded as equals in the club, ladies were not included on the Club Committee until 1948. *(Image courtesy of Donnybrook LTC)*

TODAY DONNYBROOK TENNIS Club continues to be one of the leading tennis clubs in Dublin. It has a long tradition of producing great league tennis players at junior, senior and veteran levels. It also runs a junior development programme.

DONNYBROOK
POLICE STATION

THE ROYAL IRISH Constabulary (RIC) and the Dublin Metropolitan Police (DMP) were established to replace the old County Constabulary that had existed previously. For many years there were two police stations in Donnybrook. One was the barracks of the RIC at the Donnybrook end of Belmont Avenue, and the other was the Dublin Metropolitan Police (DMP) station in the main street. It was located on the same site as the current Donnybrook Garda station, which was built in 1931, to replace the old DMP Barracks. This was also the site of the former Glebe House for St Mary's Church

of Ireland in Donnybrook Graveyard. The old police station was a three-storey masonry building removed by the Pembroke Urban District Council in 1931, when they were widening the main street in Donnybrook. G. & T. Crampton built the present Garda station and the architect was J.M. Fairweather of the Office of Public Works. Built as a granite stone-faced structure, it is a seven-bay block, and it has three bay wings. *(Image courtesy of Brian Siggins)*

TODAY THE GARDA station in Donnybrook continues to provide a high-class service to the people of Donnybrook and of Dublin 4, as it has done over the years. Great changes have been taking place in recent times regarding the organisation of An Garda Síochána, with rationalisation of premises and reorganisation of the force in general. Hours of opening have been curtailed in many Garda stations, for example, and more modern buildings are now required for a modern police force. The Minister for Defense has recently stated that 'if we are to provide an effective policing service, we must do it using modern technology and communications systems.' At the time of writing the long-term future of Donnybrook Garda Station is unknown.

DONNYBROOK TRAMS AND TRAM GARAGE

DONNYBROOK TRAMS WERE part of the major system of trams that date from about 1872 in Dublin. Started by a number of different companies, the majority of tram systems were eventually operated by the Dublin United Tramways Company, which was owned by William Martin Murphy (who had extensive business interests in the city of Dublin). All the horse-drawn trams had their own distinctively coloured cars, Donnybrook's being yellow. Two horses were used to draw the trams and the horses were changed at intervals during the day. Horse-drawn trams did not have specific stops but could be hailed by people anywhere along the road. Donnybrook trams began in O'Connell Street and continued on to the village of Donnybrook with their terminus near Donnybrook Catholic church. Electrification was first introduced in the late nineteenth century, and on 23 January 1899 electric trams were introduced on the Donnybrook routes.

Initially, destinations were printed on the side of the horse-drawn trams. In 1897 interchangeable boards were introduced, and in 1903 roller-blind destination scrolls were used. However, it was 1918 before numbers on the trams came into use. During the late nineteenth century and the early twentieth centuries trams were housed at the Donnybrook Tram Depot including the Nos 9 and 10 – the old Donnybrook trams. Two tram depots at Cabra and Donnybrook were used specifically by the Dublin United Tram Company to supply trams for cross-city services. *(Image courtesy of Danny Parkinson; horse-drawn tram image courtesy of Michael Corcoran Collection, Irish Transport Museum)*

40

TODAY, THE TRAM Garage is part of the Donnybrook bus depot and it is in use as the No. 2 Bus Garage. It is located next to the modern bus garage, on part of a disused quarry facing the River Dodder on Beaver Row. The stones from this quarry were used in the building of the Dublin to Kingstown (Dún Laoghaire) railway.

DONNYBROOK VILLAGE

FROM EARLIEST TIMES Donnybrook has featured in the annals of Irish history, initially as a place of hospitality, and then as a place of worship close to the River Dodder where St Broc is reputed to have built a convent. In the nineteenth century, industries developed in Donnybrook, such as Duffy's cotton and calico mills, a hat factory and quarries. Donnybrook seems to have been a thriving village over the centuries, though many changes have taken place since then, such as those described by W. St John Joyce in his book *The Neighborhood of Dublin* (1912): 'Donnybrook is now almost merged in the populous district around it, though still retaining its distinctive character as a village. Few of its old features, however, remain: its quaint inns are gone, its thatched cottages have vanished, and the whole place has assumed a less rural appearance than it possessed in the days when the "glories of its Fair shed around it their halo of renown".' *(Image courtesy of Brian Siggins; John Hickey image courtesy of Danny Parkinson)*

MOST OF THE shops in Donnybrook were located on both sides of Main Street. Old images of the village give some indication of the fine shops and shopping which were available to the people of Donnybrook. Unfortunately, most of these shops were demolished in the 1960s to make way for the large AIB Bank premises, which is no longer in use. There was another compulsory purchase order in the 1970s when all the shops facing the present Balloon Shop, the Ulster Bank and Bang & Olufsen were replaced by the present fire station. In addition, a row of small houses known as White's Terrace were also knocked down in the 1960s, and replaced with Donnybrook Mall, which houses a variety of different shops.

EGLINTON ROAD

EGLINTON ROAD CONTAINS a large number of houses dating back to the nineteenth century. No. 51 Eglinton Road was the home of James Franklin Fuller (1835–1924), a well-known Dublin architect who designed a number of churches throughout Ireland. Another distinguished house on Eglinton Road was Ballinguile House, which dated from 1725, and was built for Sir Robert Jocelyn, a former Solicitor General and later Lord Chancellor of Ireland (1739–1756). Ballinguile House had a name change in 1818, when it was bought by the Bower family and became known as Bowerville. It was renamed Ballinguile by Dr Wright, a member of the influential Wright family associated with the hat factory in Donnybrook. In the nineteenth century it became the property of John Henderson, who owned Henderson's Saw Mills in Donnybrook. Later it was acquired by Mr Henry Bantry White, a well-known Dublin solicitor, who gave part of its grounds to form Donnybrook Lawn Tennis Club. Another substantial house and grounds on Eglinton Road was Floraville House, which was the first Irish home of Col. Thomas Gonne, the father of Maud Gonne. Part of the land was sold for development in the 1930s, to a Mr Matthew Kirkham who built Eglinton Park on part of the land. The house itself survived until the 1960s when it was demolished to make way for a block of apartments. Garrett Fitzgerald, a former Taoiseach, lived in No. 75 Eglinton Road in a house dating from around 1879. It was from here that he launched his political career and it was here that he met subsequently with many national and international political figures. *(Image courtesy of David Crampton; Floraville House image courtesy of Danny Parkinson)*

TODAY, EGLINTON ROAD is still a road with fine substantial red-brick houses, including one particularly nice one built by Crampton's in 1910 called Fairholm. It is now called Marita. Ballinguile House is now the site of Eglinton Square, a modern housing development. However, it still retains St Broc's well in its grounds.

EVER READY GARAGE

THE EVER READY Garage was almost a Donnybrook institution. It provided motorists with a wonderful service over all the years that it existed. It was located on part of the old fair green of the Donnybrook Fair. Dating from 1927, when Johnny Reddy, Billy Dikon, and Freddy Smith founded it, the later owner, Oswald Barton, joined the firm in 1928. It was located between Brookvale Road and the main Donnybrook Road – it was always situated beside the Religious Sisters of Charity. It was only when the garage was refused planning permission to upgrade the existing garage, and they received some compensation for being refused permission, that the family bought the site behind the shops in the middle of the village and built a warehouse there. Advertisements in the late twentieth century showed it to be Ireland's Ultra-Service Station, catering for every need of the motorist. The garage specialised in the sale and servicing of Austin, Triumph, Rover, Jaguar, Mercedes, Citroen, Jensen, Lotus and Daimler cars. The garage claimed in advertisements that 'the Ever Ready reputation stands as their guarantee of reliability'. The Ever Ready Garage

closed in 1980 because, at the time, there was no member of the Barton family available to take over the business. Since then Richard Barton, a member of the next generation, has opened an Ever Ready Garage at Cross, County Mayo, specialising in classic cars. *(Image courtesy of Bob Montgomery, RAC Archivist)*

TODAY, THE SITE of the Ever Ready Garage and the area immediately surrounding it forms a triangular site and John O'Sullivan, a well-known businessman, and his family now own it. There are a number of other business on the site, including the Topaz petrol station and shop, Fast Fit Tyres and John O'Sullivan's own business, United Tyres. Plans to develop the entire site some years ago did not acquire the necessary planning permission.

FRENCH EMBASSY OFFICES

BATT O'CONNOR, A well-known builder, politician and friend of Michael Collins, originally built this house for the Humphreys family. Like other houses built by O'Connor, 36 Ailesbury Road had its secret room which Irish rebel leaders used as a hiding place when they were on the run. The Humphreys family took the Anti-Treaty side during the War of Independence and for this reason their home suffered greatly from raids by Government forces during the 1920s.

Sighle Humphreys, the owner of this house for many years, was born in Limerick to a wealthy family. She was the only daughter of a Dr David Humphreys and Mary Ellen O'Rahilly. Sighle's mother was a sister of 'The O'Rahilly' who lost his life during the 1916 Rising. Her two brothers were educated by Padraic Pearse, at St Enda's, and she herself was a boarder in the Sacred Heart School at Mount Anville. During

her lifetime Sighle Humphreys was very active politically in Cumann na mBan, where she acted as secretary for a number of years, director of publicity and national vice-president. She maintained her interest in the Republican movement all her life, and she left her family papers to the Department of Archives in University College Dublin where they are available for research purposes. *(Image courtesy of Croine and Manchán Magan)*

FORTY-SEVEN YEARS ago, No. 36 Ailesbury Road was sold to the French Embassy. Used as the Embassy offices, it was located very close to the ambassador's residence on Ailesbury Road. It was, however, recently sold by the French Government, who wished to move their staff to new premises in the centre of Dublin. It was sold to a family trust, so once again it will become a family home.

GAYFIELD/AVILA

GAYFIELD HOUSE HAD first been built as a suburban residence for a member of the Yelverton family in the eighteenth century. This family were actively involved in politics, and, in particular, with the Irish Parliament in College Green. Later Gayfield House was rented out annually, until it was sold to the Dioceses of Dublin, in 1859, as a site for a new seminary. The Dioceses also purchased Clonliffe, on the north side of the city, and it was decided to make Clonliffe the location of the Diocesan seminary instead of Gayfield. For a number of years Gayfield was a hall of residence attached to St Laurence O'Toole's Seminary in Harcourt Street. Dr William Walsh, later an Archbishop of Dublin, was one of its most distinguished alumni. A novel by Canon Sheehan called *Geoffrey Austin* provides a glimpse of Gayfield as a boarding school, surrounded by orchards and green fields.

In 1875 the Carmelite Fathers bought Gayfield, with the aid of a generous benefactor, and it opened as a House of Studies in 1884. An extension to Gayfield was built in 1886, to provide more accommodation for the Carmelite fathers. The Church at Gayfield dates from 1902, when Patrick Byrne, a well-known Dublin architect, designed it. Further additions were made to Gayfield in 1934 and 1946. Unfortunately, there is no trace of the original Gayfield House today.

GAYFIELD CHANGED ITS name to Avila in recent years when the new Avila Carmelite centre opened in 2006. The emphasis on the new centre is on a variety of retreats and spirituality courses. The centre is also used by local groups for a poetry and book club, silver screen evenings etc. There is also an Alzheimer's Café where people with dementia, their families and friends meet with health and social care professionals, for a unique blend of education and support.

THE GROVE

THE GROVE IS a bird sanctuary and it covers an enclosed area of approximately half an acre at the junction of Wellington Place and Morehampton Road. From the beginning, it has been covered in trees, shrubs, wildflowers and undergrowth. It is a wonderful home to a variety of different types of birds. The former owner of the Grove was Kathleen Goodfellow (1891–1980), daughter of a building contractor called George Goodfellow and his wife Susan. The family were Quakers, and George Goodfellow built a number of houses on Morehampton Road (Nos 2, 4, 6, 10 and 12). He retained Nos 2 and 4 for himself, and probably sold the others. Kathleen therefore inherited these houses and continued to live in No. 4 Morehampton Road until her death in 1980. Educated at Alexandra College, Kathleen then attended Trinity College Dublin from which she graduated with an Arts Degree. She loved nature and she left the Grove in trust with An Taisce – the National Trust for Ireland – in 1979.

THE GROVE TODAY is a quiet oasis amid the hustle and bustle of daily life. Many Donnybrook people are hardly aware of its existence. It is looked after by a number of volunteers under the auspices of An Taisce, who visit it regularly and replenish food supplies for the birds. Trees and shrubs are the backbone of any bird sanctuary and these are there in abundance. Bird sanctuaries are popular places and people really enjoy visiting them so a strategy is needed to acquire funding to enable the Grove to be open to the public. This would involve providing controlled access and facilities such as footpaths and seats, to allow the public to observe and photograph the birds.

HERBERT PARK

THE HISTORY OF Herbert Park goes back to an area known as the 'Forty Acres' that was part of the Fitzwilliam Estate from the 1300s. In 1816, it became the property of the Earls of Pembroke. To mark the coming of age of his son, the Hon. Sidney Herbert, the earl, offered the Forty Acres to the Pembroke Township for a public park. Plans were in hand from 1903 for an International Exhibition in Dublin, with the establishment of the International Exhibition Committee. In 1907, part of the Forty Acres was rented to the organisers of the exhibition for a rent of £1,000 per annum, for three years. Additional land was also rented from the Hippsley Estate in areas of Brendan, Argyle and Aranmore Roads. Impressive buildings were erected, and all the major countries in the British Empire were represented. There were two main entrances to the exhibition, one in Ballsbridge and one on Morehampton Road. A highlight of the exhibition was the visit of King Edward VII and Queen Alexandra on 10 July 1907. All the buildings were temporary, and were removed at the end of the exhibition. *(Image courtesy of Brian Siggins)*

TODAY, HERBERT PARK covers 32 acres and is divided in two by Herbert Park Road. The layout of the park today is similar to other late Victorian and Edwardian parks in Dublin. Herbert Park is a wonderful amenity for the people of Donnybrook, with its fine architectural features, beautiful flowerbeds and interesting pathways and walkways. It has ten different entrances, a duck pond (one of the few remaining features from the Irish International Exhibition of 1907), tennis courts, a bowling green, football pitches, a croquet lawn, synthetic sports pitch and allotments. In August 2011, the centenary of the opening of Herbert Park was celebrated with a great family day in the park.

HOME VILLAS, ST BROC'S & PEMBROKE COTTAGES

THERE WAS A sizeable working-class population in the Pembroke Township and Donnybrook in the nineteenth century, and the lack of adequate housing was a major problem. Between 1896 and 1913, 122 artisan cottages and houses were built in Donnybrook by Pembroke Urban District Council, the majority of them in Home Villas. Home Villas consists of two avenues of two-storey houses. The architect was Mr Edwin Bradbury MRIAI, and they were built for the Pembroke District Council. The formal opening of Home Villas was by Her Excellency, the wife of the Lord Lieutenant, the Countess Aberdeen. Seventy-seven houses in total were built at Home Villas. The cost to the Pembroke Council was £24,000 and the rents obtained varied from 4s 9d to 7s per week. The more expensive ones had a better location, or their rooms

were larger. Each house included a bathroom, which was most unusual for the time. The builder was a local contractor called Shortall, and Irish material was used in the main. Local labour was also employed to build the houses. As part of this development eleven one-storey cottages were built called St Broc's Cottages. A further eighty-five houses were built in the wake of the 1911 election, when the Nationalists won control of the Pembroke Urban District Council. Pembroke Cottages date from this period. Each of the individual cottages featured modern sanitary services. *(Image courtesy of the Irish Architectural Archive)*

TODAY HOME VILLAS, St Broc's and Pembroke Cottages have been extended and improved by their owners. They are all located in quiet enclaves in the heart of Donnybrook, and so are exceptionally convenient to the village and all its services. In more recent years young and trendy couples have purchased many of the houses in Home Villas and the cottages, their location in the heart of Donnybrook being very significant.

LABURNUM COTTAGE

LABURNUM COTTAGE IS one of the oldest houses in
Donnybrook, dating back to around 1710. It is located
just off Eglinton Road on Harmony Avenue. Formerly
known as San Mario, it was originally a farmhouse
surrounded by open fields as part of the Floraville estate.
At one time Floraville was occupied by Col. Gonne, the
father of Muad Gonne who spent her childhood in this
house. The cottage is a three-bay, two-storey detached
house but it has been much altered over the years, with
owners adding on additional accommodation to meet
their living needs. The house was home for a number
of years to Carey Harrison Lamb (son of Rex Harrison
and Lilli Palmer). He has written some forty plays and
sixteen novels and is now based in New York where he
is Professor of English at Brooklyn College of the City
University of New York. His father was a regular visitor
to Laburnum Cottage. It was also the home to a White

Russian princess called Lydia Prescott, who escaped from Russia in 1917, by marrying a Captain Prescott. She later married an Irish doctor. In a book called *Mariga and her Friends* by Carol Peck, two of Mariga Guinness's friends describe a picnic in Laburnum Cottage given by Mariga in honour of her friend Leda Prescott's birthday in 1979. *(Image courtesy of* The Irish Times*)*

TODAY, LABURNUM COTTAGE is a protected structure, with a preservation order on it. It has a delightful cottage garden, a patio garden and it is surrounded by a high stone wall. There is also a small studio at the bottom of the garden. It continues to be a private residence.

MARLBOROUGH ROAD

BUSHMOUNT AVENUE CHANGED its name to Marlborough Road in 1880. It was named for the Duke of Marlborough, grandfather of Sir Winston Churchill, who was Viceroy in Ireland in 1880. One cannot mention Marlborough Road without mentioning Patrick Plunkett and Patrick Cranny, well-known Dublin builders, whose wives were first cousins and very wealthy. In 1860, Patrick Cranny built a house (Muckross Park) for his wife Maria as their family home. In 1862 he also bought up all the land and houses around Muckross Park, including Sandford Avenue and Garden Cottages. When George Plunkett, Patrick Plunkett's son, married his cousin Josephine Cranny in 1884, a wealthy property dynasty was created which has lasted to the present day. During the 1860s a number of houses designed by Edward H. Carson, the father of Sir Edward Carson, were built at the Ranelagh end of the road. *(Image courtesy of Honor O'Brolchain)*

TODAY, MARLBOROUGH ROAD is still distinguished by its lovely Victorian architecture and remains a busy thoroughfare, linking Morehampton Road with Ranelagh. The earliest houses on the road are still there (Nos 47, 49 and 51), and descendants of the Plunkett and Cranny families continue to own property and live on this road. Built originally for the middle classes of the Pembroke Township, these red-brick Victorian houses were built with basements above ground level. Though designed in general to improve the living conditions of domestic staff that lived and worked in the basements, they may also have been to show that families could afford live-in staff. Today, basements in the houses on Marlborough Road are often garden flats or family kitchens. Houses on Marborough Road still contain their nineteenth-century fittings made of brass and bronze, together with mortice locks, decorative door knobs and sash windows with large glass panes.

MONTROSE

MONTROSE HOUSE WAS built in the early 1800s, and it may have been remodelled or rebuilt about 1835. From 1836 it was inhabited by the Jameson family, the well-known Dublin distillers. The house is also associated with Marconi, whose mother was a Jameson. Other occupants of Montrose were Malcolm and

Lady Ingles (Heaton's Coal), the Martin family (T & C. Martin) and a Major Vincent Kelly, who fought in the Boer War. In 1947, the house was acquired by the National University of Ireland, with a view to moving University College Dublin from Earlsfort Terrace to a greenfield site. Sometime before this, the Office of Public Works had bought Ardmore on the opposite side of the Stillorgan Road, as a future home for the National Broadcasting Station. An agreement was reached between the two bodies and a direct exchange of property took place. Montrose became the home of RTÉ, and Ardmore became part of the campus of University College Dublin. *(Image courtesy of RTÉ Stills Library)*

THE RADIO CENTRE was the first to move to Montrose and Telefís Éireann began broadcasting on New Year's Eve in 1961. Building at Montrose commenced in 1969, and the Radio Centre was completed in 1971. The main architect for the RTÉ Campus at Montrose has been the firm of Scott Tallon Walker. In the 1970s additional lands adjacent to Montrose were purchased by the RTÉ Authority to allow for expansion. New buildings on the campus included new television studios, office accommodation, and a staff canteen, which were built in the 1980s and 1990s. Montrose is still the home of RTÉ and its 360-foot television mast, built in 1960, is a well-known landmark in Donnybrook. Nowadays the old house is an administration centre.

MOREHAMPTON ROAD

FORMERLY KNOWN AS Donnybrook Road, this
road became Morehampton Road in the middle of
the 1800s. The road was part of a route that dated
back to medieval times and linked Donnybrook with
the city of Dublin. Houses along Morehampton Road
were built in the nineteenth century and are mostly
terraces of two-storey houses. A number of the houses
on Morehampton Road at the city end of the road were
built by George Goodfellow, the father of Kathleen
Goodfellow (1891–1980), who left The Grove – a bird
sanctuary – to An Taisce. Séamus Ó Súilleabháin
(James Starkey) and his wife Estella Solomons, the artist,
lived in No. 2, and Kathleen Goodfellow lived in No. 4
Morehampton Road. Estelle and Kathleen were great
friends. They were both members of Cumann na mBan
and worked together on the *Dublin Review*, edited by
Séamus Ó Súilleabháin. Another artist who lived on

Morehampton Road was the father of Beatrice Behan, wife of Brendan Behan, and his name was Cecil ffrench Salkeld. He was at the forefront of the avant-garde movement in Irish art and literature. This road was also home for many years to Ben Kiely, the well-known writer. Morehampton Road was also home to two private secondary schools that are no longer in existence – St Xavier's College for the sons of Catholic Gentlemen, and Park House School, a Protestant secondary school for girls that eventually amalgamated with Rathdown School in Dún Laoghaire.

MOREHAMPTON ROAD TODAY is a busy main road to the south of the county. Its Victorian and Edwardian houses continue to be the private homes of the professional and business classes as they were in the nineteenth and twentieth centuries. A thriving hotel is also situated there. Over the years it has been known as the Morehampton Hotel (with its familiar Tam O' Shanter Lounge), Sachs Hotel, and now the very popular Hampton Hotel.

MORRISON OBELISK

THE OBELISK AT the junction of Anglesea and Ailesbury Road is dedicated
to Arthur Morrison. Arthur Morrison (1765–1837), Lord Mayor of Dublin
from 1835–36, was an hotelier who owned Morrison's Hotel at the bottom of
Dawson Street. It was known that Charles Stewart Parnell stayed there regularly
on his visits to Dublin. The building still exists, and is known as Morrison's
Chambers. The obelisk states he was 'respected and esteemed' and there were
'few to equal, none to surpass him' – yet very little is known about him, and it
was impossible to find an image of him. *(Image courtesy of Dublin City Libraries)*

MORRISON WAS INVOLVED in a number of improvements in the infrastructure
of Donnybrook, including new roads and pathways, and the wall surrounding
the Church of the Sacred Heart. He also played a part in the construction of
the Anglesea Bridge over the Dodder in 1832, and he supported other local
developments such as the foundation of St Vincent's Hospital by Mother Mary
Aikenhead, and the establishment of St Mary's Magdalene Asylum. He became an
alderman (a member of local government) in 1808 and acted on the Grand Jury
of the County and City of Dublin from 1823. At one stage Arthur Morrison lived
in a house called Lilliputt, now known as Riversdale. It is located in the grounds
of St Ann's apartments adjacent to the Church of the Sacred Heart, Donnybrook.
In 1835 he moved to Belville, a Regency-styled cottage on the Stillorgan Road
which later became the home of the parish priest of the Church of the Sacred
Heart, Donnybrook. The house was bought in the mid-1980s by the Cosgrave
Brothers and it was divided in two – one half is Belville House and the other half
is Belville Cottage.

MOUNT EDEN ROAD

THERE ARE SOME fifty houses on Mount Eden Road that were built between 1884 and 1904. They were built on land belonging to a Captain Lewis Riall of Old Conna, County Wicklow. Like other roads in Donnybrook, the houses were built in small

terraces – sometimes four houses at a time. The distinguished Dublin architect James Franklin Fuller (1835–1924), who lived in Donnybrook (Eglinton Road), was involved in the design of at least two terraces on Mount Eden Road. He was also involved in the design of a new road that linked Morehampton Road and Belmont Avenue with Mount Eden Road. Another architect who was responsible for two other houses on Mount Eden Road was Francis Curran Caldbeck (1869–1956), who was also a civil engineer. Patricia McKenna, an authority on Mount Eden Road, has suggested that Captain Riall may have used Caldbeck's design for the two Mount Eden Road houses for four houses he built on Morehampton Road (Nos 119, 121, 123, and 125). Most of the houses built by Captain Riall were sold, but he held on to two semi-detached houses on Mount Eden Road that he let to tenants. A look at the 1901 and 1911 Irish Census indicates that the occupants of houses on Mount Eden Road were solicitors, bankers, and other professional and business families as well as people who had private means. In 1901, Captain Riall sold a field on the borders of Muckross Park to the Dominican sisters for £2,000. This field allowed the nuns to have an entrance to Muckross from Mount Eden Road. *(Image courtesy of John Holohan)*

TODAY, MOUNT EDEN Road is a quiet residential road in the heart of Donnybrook. There have not been any great changes to the houses on the road in recent years, and they continue to be occupied by professional and business families.

MUCKROSS PARK

PATRICK CRANNY, WHO was a well-known Dublin builder during the nineteenth and early twentieth centuries, built Muckross Park for his wife and family. Patrick Cranny bought the land for this house in 1849 from Joseph Leeson, 1st Earl of Milltown. While living in Muckross Park with his family, Patrick Cranny continued his thriving business of house building on Palmerston, Belgrave, Clyde, Raglan, Wellington and Marlborough Roads.

Muckross Park was built as a villa type of house, with two storeys over-basement. According to Honor O'Brolchain, a descendant of the Cranny and Plunkett families,

the house was built with four main reception rooms with double doors between two of them and they are still intact today. The hall contained a large staircase, and there were lovely mouldings on the ceilings, which can still be seen today. It is interesting that Patrick Cranny used the same quality and design of decorative elements in the smaller houses that he built on Marlborough Road twenty years later. The basement of Muckross Park would have been for servants, and it was quite generous in size, with large windows. A curved avenue surrounded by neatly kept lawns and trees led up to the main house. In addition there were paddocks and stables to the rear, with two conservatories at the side of the house.

When the new Church of the Sacred Heart was being built the Cranny family allowed local Catholics to attend Mass in their family home of Muckross Park. With the marriage of Josephine Cranny and George Plunkett, two major building families in Dublin were united. *(Image courtesy of Honor O'Brolchain)*

IN 1900, THE house was sold to the Dominican nuns, who added another storey to it in the 1930s. They also built a junior and secondary school in the grounds of Muckross Park from the 1900s. Today, the main house is used as the convent for the Dominican nuns.

MUCKROSS PARK SCHOOL

THE DOMINICAN NUNS purchased Muckross Park from Mrs Maria Cranny in 1900, as a home for St Mary's University College, which had been set up in 1886 by the nuns to offer lectures and classes to female students. During the nineteenth and early twentieth centuries women were not permitted to attend lectures at either of the universities in Dublin. With the admission of women to University College Dublin in 1909, the provision of lectures for female students was no longer necessary, so the Dominicans focused on their primary and secondary schools.

For a number of years Muckross was also a boarding school for girls. In 1907,

a dormitory was built and a new secondary school wing was added in 1925. Additional science rooms, a hostel for nuns attending University College Dublin, a junior school and a concert hall were also added. The school chapel was built in 1945 and additional land was acquired in 1949 for playing fields etc. In 1963 a new hostel for university students was completed and prefabricated classrooms were introduced in the 1980s. *(Image courtesy of Deirdre Mac Mhuna, School Archivist)*

IN 1999 THE Department of Education offered to build a new school for Muckross on a 10-acre site provided by the Dominica with first-class facilities. The Dominican nuns no longer run the school – it is now a lay school and is part of the Le Ceile Trust. The official opening of the new school took place on 19 April 2007. The future of the old school became a major problem for the Dominican Order; it was planned to open a multicultural centre with Dublin City Council there but, due to the recession, this could not become a reality. The Dominican Order then made a decision to demolish the major part of the old school, and to refurbish one wing as an apartment block for retired nuns.

NUTLEY
HOUSE

NUTLEY HOUSE DATES from around 1820 and may have been designed by the Irish architect Richard Morrison. The house was the home of Alderman George Roe, whose family owned Roe's Distillery. He was Lord Mayor of Dublin twice. Roe employed Ninian Niven, the director of the Botanic Gardens, to design a garden, park, lake and tall belvedere in the grounds. Another occupant of Nutley House was a high court judge and vice-chancellor of Trinity College, the Rt Hon. Dodgson Hamilton Madden. It was later owned by people called Lillis and Thompson, who sold 13 acres of the land to a builder, and new houses were built in what is now Nutley Park, together with new houses on the Stillorgan road. The entrance to Nutley House was then changed to Nutley Lane which, at the time, was known as Beechmount Avenue, and was more like a country lane. *(Image courtesy of Elm Park Golf & Sports Club)*

TODAY, NUTLEY HOUSE is the home of Elm Park Golf & Sports Club, one of the most distinguished golf clubs in the city of Dublin – indeed the only golf club in Dublin 4! The club was named for the place it was founded: Elm Park House, now the site of St Vincent's Hospital. In 1936 the committee acquired a lease on Nutley House from the Religious Sisters of Charity, so the club as we know it today dates from then. Golf is the prime activity of the club, but there is also a large tennis section, with outdoor courts and two indoor courts. A bridge club has also been part of Elm Park for many years. There is a club choir and a snooker section that have been in existence for over thirty years. For those with an interest in art, opera or books there are plenty of activities within the club to meet members' needs.

O'SHEA'S PUBLIC HOUSE

THERE WAS A public house at the corner of Belmont Avenue and Morehampton Road for many years. Before it became O'Shea's public house, it was Hennessey's. Patrick O'Shea (1907–1975) traded there from 1952 until he sold the business to Patrick Madigan in 1970. O'Shea was originally from Ballinaskelligs in County Kerry – a Gaeltacht area, so he was a native Irish speaker. His wife Mary Rafferty came from County Tyrone and she too was steeped in Irish culture. She graduated in Irish from University College Dublin and taught Irish in a number of different schools in Dublin. All of the O'Shea family could speak Irish, so it is not surprising that there was an Irish corner in the public house, which was inhabited by the Gaelgeori from RTÉ and primary teachers. There was also a literary corner in O'Shea's pub, and well-known Irish writers such as Brendan Behan, Patrick Kavanagh, Myles na Gopaleen,

and An Seabhac, were regular customers. Individual celebrities such as the late Elizabeth Taylor and Richard Burton were also known to have visited O'Shea's pub. Public houses in Dublin closed early on Sunday evenings so when O'Shea's closed, a fleet of cars would leave this public house for the Magic Carpet in Cabinteely, a pub outside the city limits. Bona fide pubs like the Magic Carpet could remain open until a very late hour! *(Image courtesy of Sheila O'Shea)*

TODAY THE SITE is occupied by O'Connell's restaurant, which moved there in 2010. Owned by Tom O'Connell, the emphasis in O'Connell's restaurant is on the provision of high-quality local, artisan, free-range and organic food. The restaurant is brasserie style, with an open-plan room, decorated with fern plants. Tom O'Connell personally welcomes guests to his restaurant and it is popular with the people of Dublin.

POOR CLARE MONASTERY, SIMMONSCOURT ROAD

THE POOR CLARES are a contemplative order of nuns within the Catholic Church. They were founded in 1212 by St Clare and St Francis of Assisi and follow the Rule of St Clare, which was approved by Pope Innocent IV in 1253. Life as a Poor Clare is spent in both work and prayer. They also attend Mass every day, all of their meals are taken in silence, and the Divine Office is recited daily.

The Poor Clare Monastery known as St Damien's has been on Simmonscourt Road since 1906. The centenary of the monastery was celebrated in 2006, to great acclaim. During the nineteenth century the property known as St Mary's Lodge had belonged to the McCann family. Their daughter was a Poor Clare nun, and when the nuns wanted to open a monastery in Dublin, she asked her parents if they would give St Mary's Lodge to the Poor Clare's for this purpose. The order had to obtain permission from the Archbishop of Dublin, Dr Edward J. Walshe, to open the new monastery, and this they obtained after a slight delay. It was at the suggestion of Sr

Magdalene McCann that Mother Genevieve became the abbess at St Damien's, and she held the post for some twenty-seven years. In the early years of the twentieth century the Poor Clare's received more postulants, and it became necessary to expand the facilities at St Damien's. In more recent years there has been a rationalisation of some of the Poor Clare monasteries and in 2008 the Poor Clare Community from Southampton joined the Poor Clare's at St Damien's. *(Image courtesy of the Poor Clares)*

TODAY ST DAMIEN'S Monastery is home to eight Poor Clare sisters who live, work and pray under the direction of their mother abbess, Sr Patrice.

ROYAL HOSPITAL

THE ROYAL HOSPITAL, Donnybrook was founded in 1743 as the Hospital for Incurables on the initiative of the Charitable Musical Society of Crow Street. It was 'to provide sufferers with food, shelter and relief from their distressing conditions'. Between 1743 and 1792 the hospital was in two locations, both on Townsend Street. In 1793 the hospital exchanged premises with a lock hospital located in Donnybrook. In 1887 the hospital became The Royal Hospital for the Incurables and in 1792 it moved into Buckingham House, which is still in use as part of the hospital today. Today it is simply known as the Royal Hospital, Donnybrook. Over the years the hospital has relied on charitable donations, bequests and fundraising. It is the oldest continuously operating hospital of its kind in Ireland and in the United Kingdom.

DATING FROM 1743, the Hospital's Royal Charter was amended several times and again in 1991. The current name and governance dates from then. The Royal Hospital today is an independent charity funded in the main by the Health Services Executive (HSE). The services offered are therefore provided within the public health service. There are no facilities for private patients. The Royal Hospital is governed by a Board of Management made up of governors of the hospital and up to five members of public bodies, including members of Dublin City Council. Today, the Royal Hospital specialises in the care of the elderly as well as those who are chronically ill and physically disabled. A wide range of rehabilitation services are available, as well as respite care and complex continuing care, together with day care hospital services. Clinical teams within the Royal Hospital offer treatments including medical, nursing and therapy expertise, including physiotherapy, occupational therapy, speech and language therapy, clinical psychology, nutrition and medical social work.

ST MARY'S CHURCH OF IRELAND, ANGLESEA ROAD

THE ORIGINAL CHURCH of Ireland dedicated to St Mary was located in Donnybrook Graveyard. Archbishop Comyn, Archbishop of Dublin, dedicated it to St Mary during the period 1181 to 1212. The church was rebuilt in 1726. After the new church at the junction of Anglesea Road and Simmonscourt Road opened in 1830, the old building in the Graveyard was demolished and its materials and monuments were sold – the only items of significance saved were the communion vessels, the parish registers and the baptismal font. These remain today in the modern church of St Mary on Anglesea Road.

The present church is built in the early English style of architecture. It was designed by John Semple (1801–1882), who was architect to the Board of First Fruits, for the ecclesiastical province of Dublin. Originally the church had a well-proportioned spire but this was damaged by a very bad storm in 1839 and never replaced. The church was extended in 1860, and in 1890 restoration work took place on it. Joseph Welland (1798–1860) designed an extension to St Mary's in the late nineteenth century. The oldest parish registers of St Mary's still in existence date from 1712 and are available at the Representative Church Body Library in Rathgar. *(Image courtesy of the RCB Library)*

THE CHURCH OF Ireland experienced a major decline in its numbers during the twentieth century. Like many of the churches in this country today, both Protestant and Catholic, St Mary's on Anglesea Road is suffering from non-attendance at church services. The younger generations in particular appear to have little or no interest in organised religions and one has to wonder about the future of church buildings in Ireland in general. Could they perhaps be used as local community centres?

SEAVIEW TERRACE

SEAVIEW TERRACE IS a fine terrace of three-storey Georgian houses built at the beginning of the nineteenth century. Anthony Trollope (1815–1882), the well-known author, lived in No. 5 Seaview Terrace with his wife and family from 1855 to 1859. He wrote four novels about Ireland – *The Macdermots of Ballycloran, The Landleaguers, Castle Richmond, The Kelly's and the O'Kellys*. However, it is the *Barchester Chronicles* for which he is best remembered, which he began writing during his time in Ireland.

Danesfield is another fine house on this road and today it is the residence of the German Ambassador to Ireland. During excavations for the building of this house in 1879, workmen came across a large burial mound that contained the graves of some 700 people. Dr William Frazier (1824–1899) published an account of it in the *Proceedings of the Royal Irish Academy* (1880). He concluded that this was the scene of a cold-blooded massacre during the Viking period. Buried apart from the victims was the grave of one of the leaders of the Vikings and at his feet were the skeletons of two young people. Among the grave goods was a fine Viking sword inlaid with gold and silver. It is now displayed in the National Museum of Ireland. A re-assessment of this Viking burial was carried out by Dr Elizabeth O'Brien, a professional archaeologist. Dr O'Brien suggests that Dr Frazier's description of the burial practice in the mass graves is that of normal burial practice in Ireland from about the fourth century AD. She is confident that the cemetery can now be recognised as a secular or familial cemetery of the Early Christian period, and that a single Viking burial was deposited there. *(Image courtesy of Dublin City Libraries)*

TODAY THE HOUSES on Seaview Terrace still look the same and they continue to be owned by members of the professional and business classes.

SHREWSBURY ROAD

SHREWSBURY ROAD WAS named for the Marquis of Shrewsbury in the nineteenth century. A number of different architects were involved in the design of the houses including Edwin Bradbury (1875–1948), Charles John Dunlop (*c.* 1886–1946), Henry James Lundy (1871–1961), Richard C. Orpen (1863–1938) and Silvanus Trevail (1851–1903).

One of the fine houses here is Runnymede, built at the end of the nineteenth century to a design by Richard C. Orpen. For many years the Chester Beatty Library was located on Shrewsbury Road until it moved to Dublin Castle.

Melfort (No. 19) was home from 1913 to 1923 to an interesting literary and musical family – the Starkies. Head of this family was the Rt Hon. William Starkie, a former President of University

College, Galway, the last High Commissioner for Primary Education in Ireland, and a classical scholar. His wife (May) entertained all the leading literati and musicians of the day in this house. Their children were talented musicians and were winning prizes at the Feis Ceoil in 1916. Among the children, Enid became Reader in French at Somerville College, Oxford. Her autobiography is called *A Lady's Child* (1941). Walter Starkie became Professor of Spanish at Trinity College, before setting up the British Council office in Madrid. His autobiography is called *Scholars and Gypsies* (1963). Chou Chou (Ida) Starkie was a gifted cellist, and played with many of the leading symphony orchestras, becoming Professor of Cello at the Royal Irish Academy of Music. *(Image courtesy of Peter Gleeson)*

SHREWSBURY ROAD CONTINUES to be home to the professional and business classes, many of whom are multi-millionaires. The residences of the Ambassadors of Africa, Finland and Germany are also on Shrewsbury Road. Shrewsbury Road was ranked as the sixth most expensive road in the world in 2007. The most expensive house on this road ever sold was Walford – it is reported that it made €58 million.

SIMMONSCOURT CASTLE

THE NAME SIMMONSCOURT or Smothescourt comes from a family with the surname Smothe, who were prominent in the fourteenth century in Dublin. The lands then belonged, like those of Merrion and Booterstown, to Walter de Ridelesford, a Norman knight. Thomas Smothe gave his name to Simmonscourt, and the 'green of Smothescourt' was popular with the people of Dublin on festive occasions. There was a bridge across the River Dodder known as the Bridge of Simmonscourt at the beginning of the seventeenth century. The bridge was in poor condition during the sixteenth century and eventually Dublin Corporation voted that £10 be taken from the city funds, to repair and improve the bridge. During the 1641 rebellion the lands of Simmonscourt were described as being

laid waste. William Fitzwilliam lived in Simmonscourt after the Restoration, but it seems that by the end of the seventeenth century Simmonscourt Castle was a ruin, and the Nossom family, who were tenants of Christ Church Cathedral, held the lands.

At the beginning of the eighteenth century a house called Simmons-court was built. It was the home, at the time of his death in 1734, of Arthur Forbes, 2nd Earl of Granard, the father of the distinguished naval commander and diplomatist, who succeeded him in the title as 3rd Earl. During the eighteenth century, a house named Ball's House was built at Simmonscourt and this was in use until 1734. At the beginning of the twentieth century the modern Simmonscourt Castle belonged to the McCann family. *(Image courtesy of the National Library of Ireland)*

TODAY ON THE lands of Simmonscourt there are a number of exclusive modern developments of both houses and apartments, located behind electronic gates. It is a private and well-established development, with lovely landscaped communal gardens. *(Image courtesy of the Archaeological Consultancy Services)*

SWANBROOK HOUSE

SIR GUSTAVUS HUME, who was a substantial landowner in Donnybrook, owned Swanbrook in the late eighteenth century. He also owned a good deal of property in the city of Dublin, where Hume Street is named after him. In 1786 he leased land to George Cowen, a glazier from Dublin, and he erected a house on the site that he named Swanbrook, after the river of the same name that ran through the grounds. Swanbrook House was probably remodelled, if not rebuilt, at the beginning of the nineteenth century. Alderman Frederick Darley, a former Lord Mayor of Dublin and member of the Corporation who also served as High Sheriff and held other public offices, also owned it. Thomas Steel, James Lindsay, Revd John Chute and his son Arthur later occupied the

house in succession. In the 1860s the property came into the hands of Colonel Edward Wright, who leased it to Bloomfield Trustees in 1863. The Society of Friends (Quakers) owned Swanbrook House for many years. Its history was similar to that of Bloomfield House, also owned by the Society of Friends. Bloomfield Hospital, New Lodge (nursing care), Swanbrook and Westfield (residential home), together with the administrative offices of the Society of Friends, all moved to Stocking Lane in Rathfarnham in 2005. *(Image courtesy of the Society of Friends)*

SWANBROOK HOUSE WAS restored recently, and is now a family residence within its own grounds. The house has also a preservation order on it. There is also a new development of exclusive houses and apartments called Edward Square that now occupies 4.85 acres of grounds belonging to Bloomfield and Swanbrook Houses. Edward Square was planned and designed to be one of the most prestigious and exclusive developments to be built in recent years. The houses and apartments are built within a landscape of a private garden square.

WESLEYAN METHODIST CHURCH

THE WESLEYAN METHODIST Church on Beaver Row was built by Joseph Wright and his brothers (James and Robert), who also built a hat factory on the River Dodder at the beginning of the nineteenth century. Joseph Wright (*d.* 1877) and his wife Mary (*d.* 1828) and their eldest daughter (*d.* 1869) are buried in Donnybrook Graveyard. Dating from around 1826, the church together with a hall and school, were built to serve their employees who had come from the north of England and who were mainly Wesleyan Methodists. The date of the closure of the hat factory has not been possible to ascertain, but it may have closed in or around the time that the Wesleyan Methodist Church closed. According to the Wesley Historical Society Dublin Archive, 'the exact date of its closure cannot be confirmed. However, it looks as though it was not used after June 1850 which is the last time it is referred to in the preaching plan of the Dublin South circuit'. *(Image courtesy of Glenda Cimino; Associated Felt Makers image courtesy of the National Library)*

THE CHURCH TODAY is located in the back garden of a private house on Beaver Row. This is one of the many cottages originally built by the Wright Brothers for their employees. These cottages, on the outside, look very much like they did when they were built in the nineteenth century, though many have been modernised to cater for twenty-first-century living. The present owner of No. 9 Beaver Row is Glenda Cimino, an American writer, who has acquired a preservation order on the church and is presently working on its restoration. The National Library holds a copy of a membership card for the Associated Felt Makers of Donnybrook, established in 1813.

WOODSIDE

THOM'S DIRECTORY, WHICH began in the
nineteenth century is an excellent source of
information about Dublin's roads and houses. One of
Donnybrook's finest roads is Shrewsbury Road and it
first appeared in *Thom's Directory* in 1886. The house
known as Woodside first appears in the 1904 issue
of the *Directory*, and by the 1905 volume of *Thom's*,
there were thirteen houses on this road, together
with a number of building sites. Woodside was built
in 1902, and the architect was the Cornish architect
Silvanus Trevall (1851–1903). It is interesting to
note that the original architectural drawings for
Woodside are still in existence in the Library of the
Representative Church Body.

The first occupants of Woodside were members of
the Parkes family who lived there until 1926, when
it was sold to the Church of Ireland, as a palace for
the Archbishop of Dublin. The first archbishop to
reside there was Revd John Allen Fitzgerald Gregg
(1873–1961), who continued to live in this house

until he became Archbishop of Armagh in 1939. Archbishop Gregg was succeeded as Archbishop of Dublin by the Revd Arthur William Barton (1881 –1962), who lived in Woodside until 1951. *(Image courtesy of Pharmaceutical Society of Ireland)*

WOODSIDE WAS BOUGHT by the Pharmaceutical Society of Ireland in 1951, and many of today's pharmacists qualified there. The Pharmaceutical Society rented Woodside to Trinity College Dublin until 1998, when it was decided to sell some of its grounds and new residences were built on part of this ground.

In 2008, Woodside was put on the market by the Irish Pharmaceutical Society for €25 million, but it took three years to sell at a figure believed to be in the region of €8 million. The buyer was a venture capitalist whose company, Ballyroan Residential Ltd, now owns it, and plans are in hand to return it to use as a family residence once again.

ABOUT THE AUTHOR & PHOTOGRAPHER

DR BEATRICE DORAN grew up in Donnybrook and still lives there. She was educated at Muckross and University College Dublin. A librarian by profession, Beatrice has worked in a number of academic and university libraries in Ireland. She is a former director of the Royal College of Surgeons in Ireland Library and past president of the Library Association of Ireland. During her years working in UCC Library she was active in the Cork Historical & Archaeological Society as vice president, council member and honorary organiser. Today she is a member of the Ballsbridge, Donnybrook & Sandymount Historical Society, the Irish Georgian Society, the Royal Society of Antiquaries and the Royal Dublin Society.

VINCENT CLARKE'S career began in his father's photograph practice in Kells, County Meath, followed by four years with Bill Crimmins in Drogheda while studying photography at the DIT (Kevin Street). He joined RTÉ Lighting Department in the late 1970s and worked as lighting director on many large productions before retiring in 2012. Vincent has extensive knowledge and experience of digital photography with particular emphasis on composition and lighting. For further examples of his work see www.vclarkephoto.com.